Learn and Play with

Jesus and Me Every Day

The Promised Gift

"For God loved the world so much that he gave his only Son"

John 3:16

Karyn Henley

CWR, Waverley Abbey House, Waverley Lane, Farnham, Surrey GU9 8EP

National Distributors

UK (and countries not listed below): CWR, PO Box 230, Farnham, Surrey GU9 8XG. Tel: (01252) 784710   Outside UK (44) 1252 784710

AUSTRALIA: CMC Australasia, PO Box 519, Belmont, Victoria 3216. Tel: (03) 5241 3288

CANADA: CMC Distribution Ltd, PO Box 7000, Niagara on the Lake, Ontario L0S 1J0. Tel: (0800) 325 1297

GHANA: Challenge Enterprises of Ghana, PO Box 5723, Accra. Tel: (021) 222437/223249   Fax: (021) 226227

HONG KONG: Cross Communications Ltd, 1/F, 562A Nathan Road, Kowloon. Tel: 2780 1188 Fax: 2770 6229

INDIA: Crystal Communications, 10-3-18/4/1, East Marredpally, Secunderabad – 500 026. Tel/Fax: (040) 7732801

KENYA: Keswick Bookshop, PO Box 10242, Nairobi. Tel: (02) 331692/226047

MALAYSIA: Salvation Book Centre (M) Sdn Bhd, 23 Jalan SS 2/64, 47300 Petaling Jaya, Selangor.
Tel: (03) 78766411/78766797 Fax: (03) 78757066/78756360

NEW ZEALAND: CMC New Zealand Ltd, Private Bag, 17910 Green Lane, Auckland. Tel: (09) 5249393 Fax: (09) 5222137

NIGERIA: FBFM, Helen Baugh House, 96 St Finbarr's College Road, Akoka, Lagos. Tel: (01) 7747429/4700218/825775/827264

PHILIPPINES: OMF Literature Inc, 776 Boni Avenue, Mandaluyong City. Tel: (02) 531 2183 Fax: (02) 531 1960

REPUBLIC OF IRELAND: Scripture Union, 40 Talbot Street, Dublin 1. Tel: (01) 8363764

SINGAPORE: Campus Crusade Asia Ltd, 315 Outram Road, 06-08 Tan Boon Liat Building, Singapore 169074. Tel: (065) 222 3640

SOUTH AFRICA: Struik Christian Books, 80 MacKenzie Street, PO Box 1144, Cape Town 8000. Tel: (021) 462 4360 Fax: (021) 461 3612

SRI LANKA: Christombu Books, 27 Hospital Street, Colombo 1. Tel: (01) 433142/328909

TANZANIA: CLC Christian Book Centre, PO Box 1384, Mkwepu Street, Dar es Salaam. Tel: (051) 2119439

UGANDA: New Day Bookshop, PO Box 2021, Kampala. Tel: (041) 255377

ZIMBABWE: Word of Life Books, Shop 4, Memorial Building, 35 S Machel Avenue, Harare. Tel: (04) 781305 Fax: (04) 774739

For e-mail addresses, visit the CWR web site: www.cwr.org.uk

Tails: The Promised Gift

© 2001 Karyn Henley. All rights reserved. Exclusively administered by Child Sensitive Communication, LLC

Text and characterisations by Karyn Henley

Models created by: Debbie Smith
Photographed by: Roger Walker
Illustrator: Sheila Anderson Hardy of Advocate
Designer and line art illustrator: Christine Reissland at CWR
Editor: Lynette Brooks
Printed in England by Linney Print
ISBN 1 85345 176 2
Published 2001 by CWR

Welcome to *Tails*! *Tails* is written especially for young children, because of their unique needs and interests. Young children are strongly affected by story. So the *Tails* series presents not only Bible stories, but application stories and activities using animal characters. Young children will grow to love and identify with these animal friends. In return, the *Tails* characters will help introduce young children to the Bible, to God, and to godly values.

Each book in the *Tails* series focuses on a simple theme and memory verse that are meaningful to the young child. Using one page a day, the parent, teacher or caregiver can take the child through an entire month of theme-related scriptures, devotional thoughts, and fun activities. We suggest that as you participate in personal or family daily devotions, you include your child by guiding him or her through a page of the *Tails* book.

Of course, you may wish to use the *Tails* books as a supplement to Sunday school lessons. You may also use them as fun, Bible-based activity books for occasions when the child travels, or is sick in bed, or otherwise needs the companionship of his *Tails* friends.

We are confident that your young child will enjoy *Tails*. It is our privilege and pleasure to provide this enjoyable way for your child to grow in knowing and loving God.

By God's grace, to His glory,

Karyn Henley

Meet the Tails Friends

Welcome to Tails Town. You'll see that each of us has a different kind of tail. We have other kinds of tales, too: the stories we tell. Our favourite stories are about God. He has given each of us different tails to wear and different tales to tell. That reminds us that even though we are all different, we can work together and love each other. And that pleases God.

Mimi

Hi, friends! My name is Mimi. Let me paint my name for you. What colour? Hmmmm. All the colours of the rainbow! If I painted your name, what colour would you want me to use? I like all kinds of art. I like to paint and draw and make all kinds of crafts. If you ever want to find me, look for me in my art corner!

Owlfred

Hulloo–oo–oo! My name is Owlfred. I'm an explorer. I like to find out how things work or why things sound or feel or look the way they do. So I like to do experiments. I try things to find out what will happen. I'll help you to find things out too. Or I might give you a puzzle or ask a question to find out what YOU think.

Chester

What's up, new friends? My name's Chester. Do you like FUN? Then come with me! If there's an adventure around, I'm ready to jump right in. I love all kinds of games. If you'd like, I'll make up some games just for you. So come on along and have some FUN.

Tennyson

Ahoy there! Tennyson is my name, and I'm a poet.
   I write poems and rhymes.
   And songs sometimes.
   See there? I knew it.
   Somehow I just do it.
If you sit quietly with me, we'll see sights and hear sounds and feel our feelings. Then I'll write a poem for you. And you can write a poem for me.

Mrs H

Hello! I'm Mrs H. Are you ready for a snack? Whenever you're hungry, come into my kitchen. You'll always find something good to eat there. I'll show you how to make some of the yummiest treats you ever tasted. At least, Twigs thinks they're yummy.

Twigs

Mmmm! Yes! Are the treats ready to eat now? My name is Twigs, and I need to pack a snack for the day, because I'm going to explore with Owlfred. Then I want to watch Mimi paint. And I might play a game with Chester. Then I'll rest by the pond with Tennyson, and we'll write a song about my busy day.

Yes, it's a busy day in Tails Town! Turn the page and join us!

1 A Promise for Bethlehem

A long time ago there lived a man named Micah. Micah loved God. God told Micah something very important. God said, "Oh Bethlehem, you are just a small town. But a King will come from you. All over the world, people will say good things about Him. And He will bring peace" (Micah 5:2, 4, 5). This was God's promise to send someone special to Bethlehem.

WHOO-OO-OO
can say the verse?

"For God loved the world so much that he gave his only Son."

John 3:16

Mimi has drawn a picture of what a house in the town of Bethlehem might have looked like. Beside it, draw a picture of the place where you live. How is it the same? How is it different? What was God going to send to Bethlehem?

Mimis Art Corner

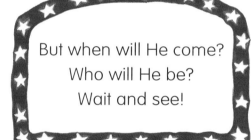

But when will He come?
Who will He be?
Wait and see!

Which is different?

Here are some Bethlehem houses. Which house is different from the others?

An Advent Wreath

Advent is a special time of waiting before Christmas comes. While they wait for Christmas, many people like to light candles to help them remember the promised King that would come to Bethlehem.

Mrs H helped Twigs make an advent wreath to hold their candles. You can make one too.

- Mix 2 cups of flour, $^1/_2$ cup of salt and $^3/_4$ cup of water.

- Roll some of the dough into a log shape. Then curve it around, and stick the ends together to make a ring.

- Use a small purple or dark blue candle to make four holes around the top of the wreath.

- Bake the wreath (but not the candle) at 250 degrees F (120 degrees C) for 20–30 minutes until it is hard.

Let the wreath cool. Then you can paint it with acrylic paints or markers.

Twigs knows he must let his mum light the candle. You must let a grown-up light your candle too. And be sure to blow it out if no one is going to be in the room with it. Keep it in a safe place.

- Set the purple or dark blue candle into one of the holes in the wreath. You will add more candles later.

- Use the leftover dough to make Christmas ornaments.

A Prayer

**Dear God,
Thank You for Your promise to send someone special to Bethlehem. Amen.**

God with us

Long ago there was a man named Isaiah. He loved God. God told Isaiah about His special promise. God said, "Watch and wait. The young woman will have a baby! She will have a son, a baby boy. He will be Emmanuel which means 'God with us'" (Isaiah 7:14). God had promised Micah that someone special would come to Bethlehem. Now God promised Isaiah that a young woman would have this baby boy who would be "God with us".

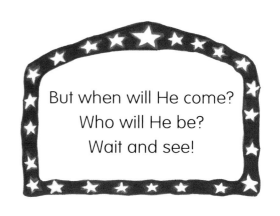

But when will He come?
Who will He be?
Wait and see!

Which is which?

Which one is a son? Which one is a daughter?

A son is a boy. A daughter is a girl. Are you a son or a daughter? Are there other children at your house? Which ones are sons? Which ones are daughters?

Draw their faces in the circles below.

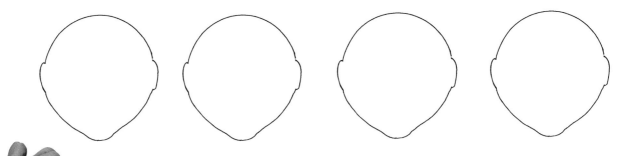

Dear God,
Thank You for Your promise to send a special Son
to be "God with us". Amen.

A Sock Baby

4

Twigs is playing with a sock baby that his mum made for him. If you want to make a sock baby, follow her directions.

- Get one child's sock or baby's sock (with no holes in the toe).

- Stuff cotton wool balls into the toe of the sock so that it makes a soft ball.

Loosely tie the sock into a knot beneath the ball to keep the cotton wool in.

- Cut one hole on each side of the ankle of the sock close to the knot.

- Draw a face on the ball of the sock baby. Your baby will need two eyes, a nose, a mouth and some rosy cheeks.

- Now put your hand into the sock, pushing your pointer finger through the loose knot and sticking your thumb and little finger out of the holes in the sock to make the baby's arms.

Here's a song I wrote for you to sing as you rock your baby. Sing it to the tune of "Frere Jacques".

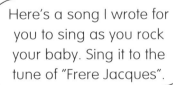

Here's a baby, here's a baby,
Little One, Little One,
God's own special promise,
God's own special promise,
Little Son, Little Son.

God had told Micah part of His promise: Someone special would come to Bethlehem. God had told Isaiah part of His promise: A young woman would have a son, a baby boy, to be "God with us". Then God told Isaiah another part of the promise. God said, "A child is born. A Son is given. He will be called Wonderful, Counsellor, Mighty God, Everlasting Father, Prince of Peace" (Isaiah 9:6).

Wonderful Names

Use a crayon to trace over this name that God said His Son would be called.

But when will He come?
Who will He be?
Wait and see!

Mighty

Now show Twigs how to write your name in the space below. Or ask someone to write it for you, and you can trace over the letters.

Whoo-oo-oo remembers the verse?

"For God loved the world so much that he gave his only Son."

John 3:16

Waiting

All our Tails friends are waiting for Christmas to come. They know it's easier to wait if they do something interesting while they're waiting. Draw a line from the Tails friends to what they will need for their ideas.

Make Christmas cards.

Wrap presents.

Take a box of food to someone needy.

Bake Christmas biscuits.

Decorate the house.

Make a snowman.

Dear God,
Please help me to find good things to do while I wait for Christmas. Amen.

A Wise King

Jeremiah loved God. One day God told Jeremiah, "A time is coming when I will send a wise King. He will do what is right and fair. He will save My people. He will be called the Lord" (Jeremiah 23:5–6). Now people knew more of God's promise. Someone special would come to Bethlehem. He would be a son born to a young woman. He would be called Wonderful and Prince of Peace. And He would be a King called the Lord.

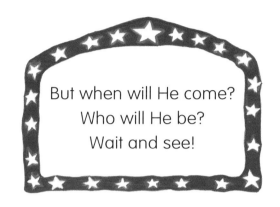

But when will He come?
Who will He be?
Wait and see!

Chester's Challenge

Stack the Kings

Turn lots of paper cups upside down. Draw a face on each cup, and pretend that each cup is a king. Now try stacking the cups in a pyramid shape like Chester has done. To make the stack higher, you have to add more cups to the bottom row. See how high you can go before the stack falls. To make the game more fun, set one king on his head. Stack the next king right side up on top of the rim of the first. Stack the next one on his head again, and so on. Try to keep them balanced!

A Prayer

Dear God,
Thank You for Your promise to send a wise King to Bethlehem for us. Amen.

It's time to put another purple or dark blue candle in your advent wreath. Purple is a colour for kings. It makes us think of the King that God promised to send to Bethlehem a long time ago. Can you guess who this King is?

A Candle Quiz

Look at the candles below. Which one is the tallest? Which is the shortest? Which is the widest (or fattest)? Which is the most narrow or thin?

Now colour the candles so that they look like Christmas candles.

Hide the Candle

Chester and Twigs like to play Hide the Candle. You can play too. Here's how. Chester gets a candle. But he doesn't light it. Twigs closes his eyes. Chester hides the unlit candle. Then he says, "A candle is hiding. Open your eyes. Where is it hiding? It's a surprise!" Then Twigs looks for the candle. When Twigs gets close to the candle, Chester says, "It's getting brighter!" When he's far from the candle, Chester says, "It's getting darker." When Twigs finds the candle, it's his turn to hide it and Chester's turn to look for it.

Baby John

Do you remember God's promises? God promised to send a baby King to Bethlehem. But a long time passed, and the promised King had not come. Then one day something very surprising happened. A man named Zechariah went to the worship house, and there he saw an angel! The angel said, "Zechariah, you and your wife Elizabeth will have a special baby. Name him John. He will get people ready for God's promised King." (Luke 1:5–25)

But when will He come?
Who will He be?
Wait and see!

Can you see it?

Help Mimi connect all the dots to see what Zechariah saw.

God made some trees to turn red or yellow when the weather grows cold. Then the leaves fall off. But other trees stay green all winter long. Why? The trees that lose their leaves need to rest and save up water during the winter so they can grow new leaves and flowers and even fruit the next year. Most of these trees have big leaves. They are called deciduous trees. Most trees that keep their leaves have thin needle-shaped leaves. They are called evergreens. Can you guess why?

Which branch has broad leaves? Which has needle-shaped leaves? Which ones do we usually use to decorate at Christmas time? Why?

Which tree below has lost its leaves? Which trees might get snow on them? Which tree would probably not get snow on it? Why?

Evergreens make us think of living for**ever** with God.

The Angel's News

Mary was a young woman who loved God. One day she got a big surprise. An angel came to see her! She had never seen an angel before. So she was scared. But the angel was good and kind. "Don't be afraid," he said. "God sent me to tell you that you will have a baby. He will be God's Son. You must name Him Jesus." Mary was excited. She knew about God's promise from long ago. Now God was going to keep His promise. And she would be the young woman who would have the special baby boy, God's Son! (Luke 1:26–38)

Now you know who the baby will be. But when will He come? Wait and see!

How many Angels?

Our Tails friends have been decorating Christmas trees. Each tree should have four angels on it.

How many more angels does Tennyson's tree need?

How many more angels does Chester's tree need?

How many more angels does Mrs H's tree need?

A Prayer

Dear God,
Thank You for keeping Your promise to send Your Son.
Amen.

Whoo-oo-oo remembers the verse?

"For God loved the world so much that he gave his only Son."

John 3:16

Mimi's Art Corner

Mimi is making angels to put on her Christmas tree. You can make some too. Use paper plates or ask someone to cut circles out of paper for you.

- Cut each paper plate or circle in half.

- Cut one of the halves in half again.
  (This makes one-quarter of a circle.)

- Lay one half down with the curved edge facing you.

- Glue or tape the other halves on top of it, leaving the curves showing from underneath.

- Glue or tape the two smaller pieces on top with their points facing away from you.

- Draw an angel face on the top piece.

- You could glue some gold or silver glitter on the wings to make them sparkle.

- Punch a hole in the top and thread ribbon or wool through it to hang it.

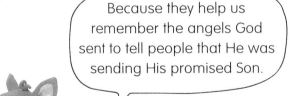

Because they help us remember the angels God sent to tell people that He was sending His promised Son.

Why do we decorate with angels at Christmas?

Mary takes a trip

Mary had a special secret. She was going to have a baby, God's own Son. Mary hurried to the hill country to tell Elizabeth. Elizabeth was going to have baby John. As soon as Mary said "Hello", baby John jumped for joy inside Elizabeth. "God has blessed you," said Elizabeth. "Yes," said Mary. Then Mary was so happy that she sang a song of love and thanks to God. "Oh, how I praise the Lord," sang Mary. "He has done great things for me!" (Luke 1:39–56)

Now you know who the baby will be.
But when will He come?
Wait and see!

Which Comes Next?

Tennyson writes songs. He writes the words of the songs with letters. But he writes the music of the songs with notes. Look at these notes. Show Tennyson which note should come next by drawing it in the space.

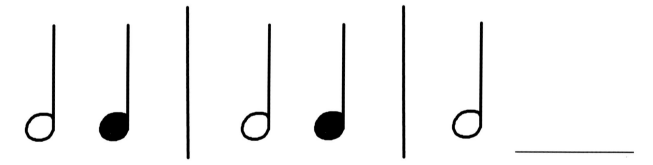

We call Christmas songs "carols". What are some of your favourite Christmas carols?

Do you know a carol about  ?   Do you know a carol about ?

Do you know a carol about  ?   Do you know a carol about  ?

**Dear God,
I praise You just as Mary did. You have done great things! Amen.**

Why do we eat lots of good food with our friends at Christmas time?

It's a way of celebrating and enjoying the good things God has given us.

From Mrs H's Kitchen

Eating lots of good food is called feasting. Twigs especially likes to help make gingerbread people at Christmas time. He calls them "ginger people". You can make them too.

Ginger People

$^{1}/_{2}$ cup sugar

$^{1}/_{2}$ cup margarine

$^{1}/_{2}$ cup treacle

$^{1}/_{4}$ cup water

$2^{3}/_{4}$ cups flour plus extra flour

$^{3}/_{4}$ teaspoon salt

$^{3}/_{4}$ teaspoon ground ginger

$^{1}/_{2}$ teaspoon baking powder

$^{1}/_{4}$ teaspoon cinnamon

Beat the sugar, margarine, treacle and water in a large bowl. Add flour, salt, ginger, baking soda, and cinnamon. Chill the dough in the refrigerator for at least 1 hour. Then preheat the oven to 345 degrees F (180 degrees C). Pat the dough flat. Cut it out with people-shaped biscuit cutters. Bake for 6 to 8 minutes. Decorate with sweets and icing if you wish.

A night in Bethlehem

Clip-clop, clip-clop, down the road went the donkey, carrying Mary on its back. Mary was going to have her baby soon. But first, she and her husband Joseph had to go to Bethlehem. They had to be counted with all the other families who had lived there long ago. Bethlehem was busy and crowded with people when Mary and Joseph got there. So when they asked for a place to stay, everyone said "No room". Where could they stay? There was only one place: in a stable with donkeys and cows and chickens and goats! (Luke 2:1–5)

Here is an inn, a hotel, in the town of Bethlehem. There was no room left in the inn.
So draw a face of someone looking out of each window.
Where did Mary and Joseph stay?

Packing

Twigs is going to spend the night at Chester's house. What should he pack in his bag?

It's time to put another candle in your advent wreath.
This time put a rose or pink coloured candle in it. This colour means joy. It reminds us of how happy we are that God sent His Son, Jesus.

Cwlfred's Experiment

Empty and Full

Put a towel on a tray or on the table where you're going to do your experiment. Place a cup with nothing in it onto the towel. Is the cup empty or full? It's full of air. But it's empty of anything else. Now fill it with water until it's full but not spilling over. Lower your head so that your eyes are looking right across the rim of the cup from the side. Now drop one small coin into the water. The water level gets higher. Keep dropping coins into the water, one at a time, until you see the water rise up, curving above the rim of the cup. At first the water seems to be held together and does not spill out. But add another coin. How many coins did you put into the cup before the water spilled out?

All the houses in Bethlehem were already full of people when Mary and Joseph got to town. Where did they have to stay?

A Prayer

Dear God,
Thank You for Mary and Joseph. Thank You for giving them a place to stay. Amen.

God keeps His promise

Bethlehem's houses were full, and even though there was room in the stable, it wasn't empty. There were dozy donkeys, snuffling cows, gruffy goats, chatty chickens, and maybe even a family of scurrying mice. In the middle of all the snuffling and snorting and clucking and scratching, there came a very different sound: a baby crying. Mary's baby had been born. Mary wrapped the tiny baby in some cloth to keep Him warm and cosy. Then she laid Him in the hay in a manger. God had kept His promise to send His Son to Bethlehem! (Luke 2:1–7)

Tennyson's Rhyme Time

Tennyson has written a poem about the stable. Read it by saying the word for the picture.

Oats for the   .

The   eats   .

The   is the place

Where the   stay.

That's where

Was born on Christmas   .

In the   in   .

Do you Remember?

The angel had told Mary to name her baby "Jesus".
So she did.

Sweet Stripes

Colour these candy canes with the number of stripes that are written below them.

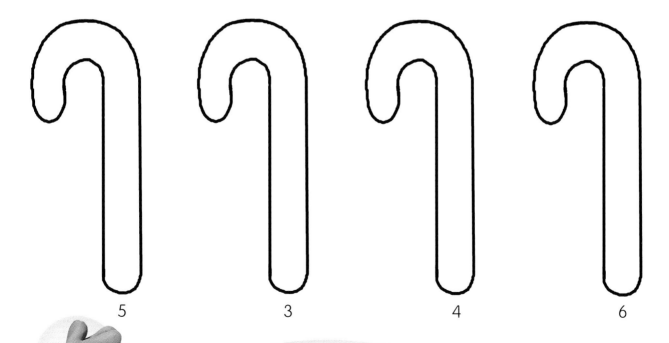

5   3   4   6

A Prayer

Dear God,
Thank You for sending Baby Jesus. Thank You for keeping
Your promise. Amen.

News for the shepherds

On the night that Baby Jesus was born, there were shepherds out in the fields. They were watching their sheep. Suddenly an angel came right into the field with them. And God's bright glory shone all around them. The shepherds were scared. But the angel said, "Don't be afraid. I have good news for you. God's Son was born today in Bethlehem!" Then lots of angels came, praising God. "Glory to God in the highest!" they said. When the angels left, the shepherds said, "Let's go and see this new baby." They hurried to Bethlehem and found Baby Jesus in a manger in the stable. Then the shepherds praised God. He had sent His Son Jesus! (Luke 2:8–20)

Angels and Sheep All Around

Here is a shepherd watching sheep. Colour a bright light of God's glory shining down from the sky.

Which sheep is beside the shepherd? Which is going away from the shepherd? Which is behind something? Which is on top of something? What is above the shepherd and the sheep?

Dear God,
The angels praised You. The shepherds praised You. I praise You too. Glory to You, God! Amen.

Why do we hear bells at Christmas time?

Because bells ring to give us news. Some bells tell what time it is. Some tell us that dinner is ready. Christmas bells help us remember the good news that the angels told the shepherds: Jesus is born!

Owlfred's Experiment

God has given us ears to hear His news.

Drop a grain of uncooked rice into a bowl of water. Watch the ripples. The rice sent out rippling waves in the water. Sounds send out rippling waves in the air. We can't see the waves. But they hit our ear drums, and we hear the sound they carry. Thread a string about 60cm long through an old metal key or lid. Cover your ears and ask a friend to bump the key onto the edge of a table, holding the ends of the string. What do you hear?

The sound waves can't get to your ears very well. Now with one end of the string in each hand, put the string ends into your ears. Hold the string in your ears while you bump the key or lid against the table again. What do you hear? The sound waves travelled through the string and went right to your ears, making the sound quite loud!

What sound did the shepherds hear on the night when Baby Jesus was born?

News from a star

High in the sky was a very special star. Down on the ground were some very special wise men, watching the sky. "Look at that star!" they said. "It is a sign. It means that a baby King has been born. Let's go and find the baby King and worship Him!" So they travelled over straight roads and winding roads, over hills and valleys, across rivers and fields. At last they came to a big city where a big king lived. "Where is the new baby King?" the wise men asked. But the big king didn't know. He asked his helpers. His helpers knew the words of Micah. So they said, "God told Micah that He would send a King to Bethlehem." "Then that's where we'll go," said the wise men. And off they went to find the baby King. (Matthew 2:1–8)

Mimi's Art Corner

The wise men probably rode on camels. To finish this camel, cover the bottom of an old plate with paint. Make a fist. Press the side of your fist onto the paint and then onto the camel. Point your knuckles towards the top of the page so the fist print will make a hump for the camel.

Whoo-oo-oo remembers the verse?

"For God loved the world so much that he gave his only Son."

John 3:16